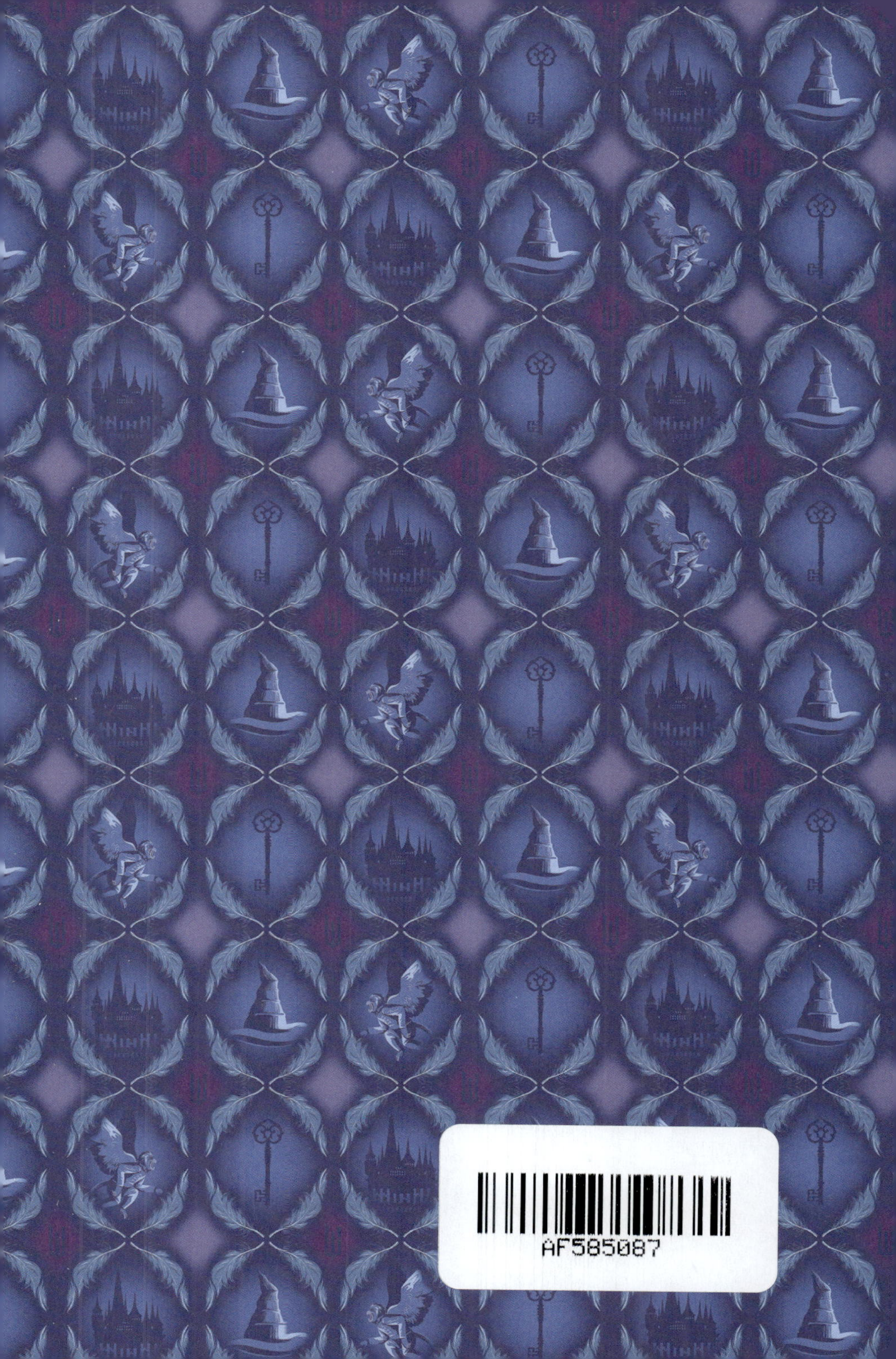
AF585087

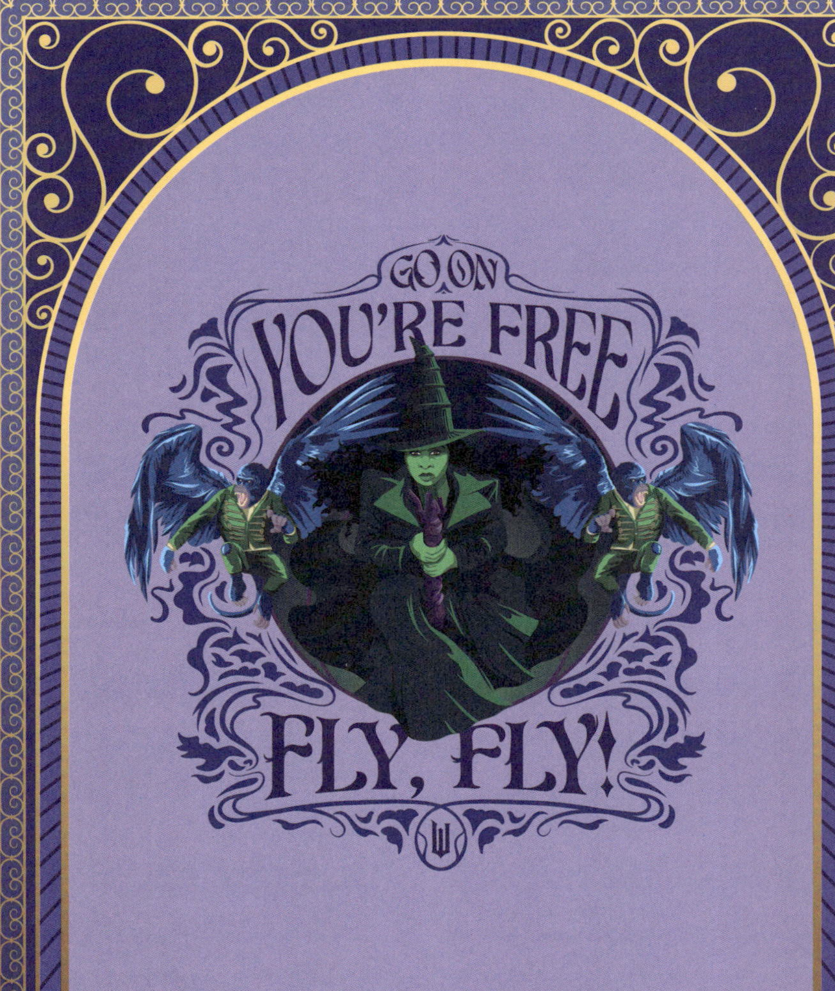
GO ON
YOU'RE FREE
FLY, FLY!

THIS BELONGS TO

____

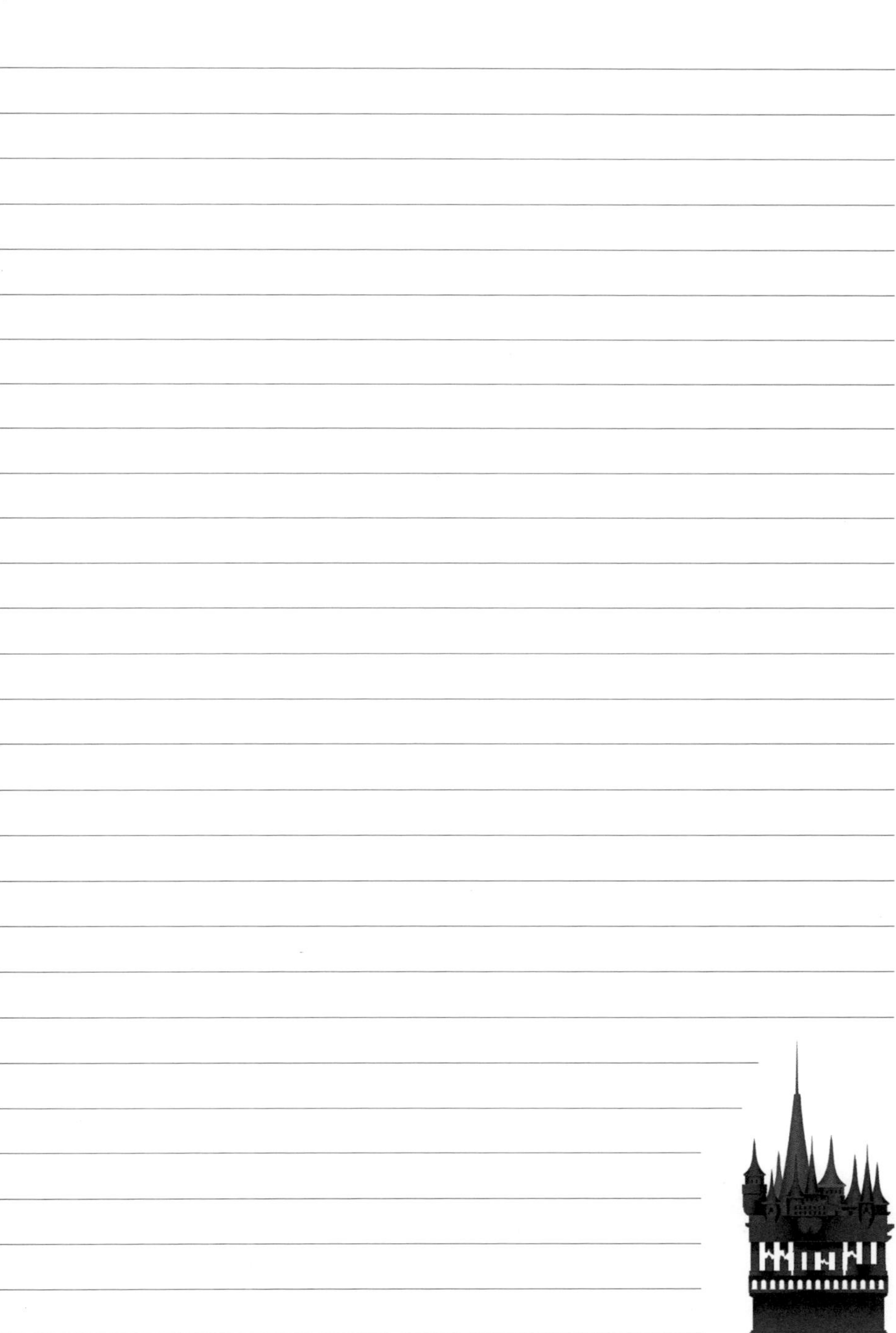

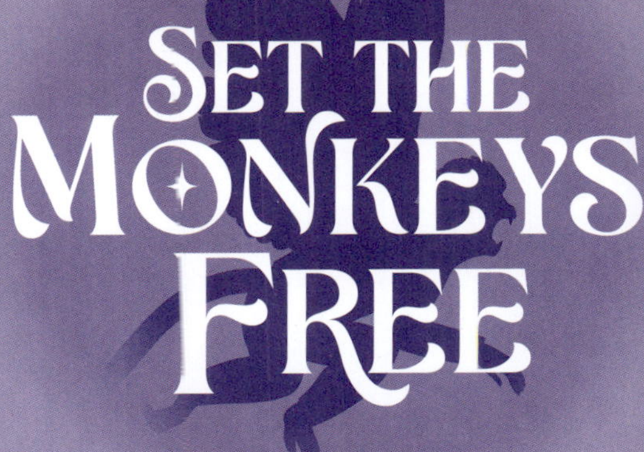
SET THE
MONKEYS
FREE

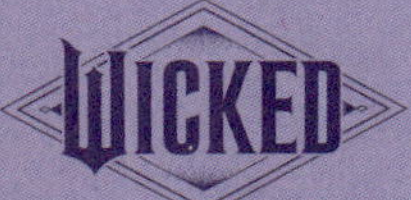
WICKED

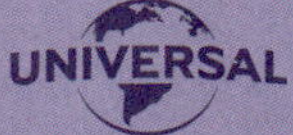
UNIVERSAL

INSIGHTS
insighteditions.com

MANUFACTURED IN CHINA
10 9 8 7 6 5 4 3 2 1

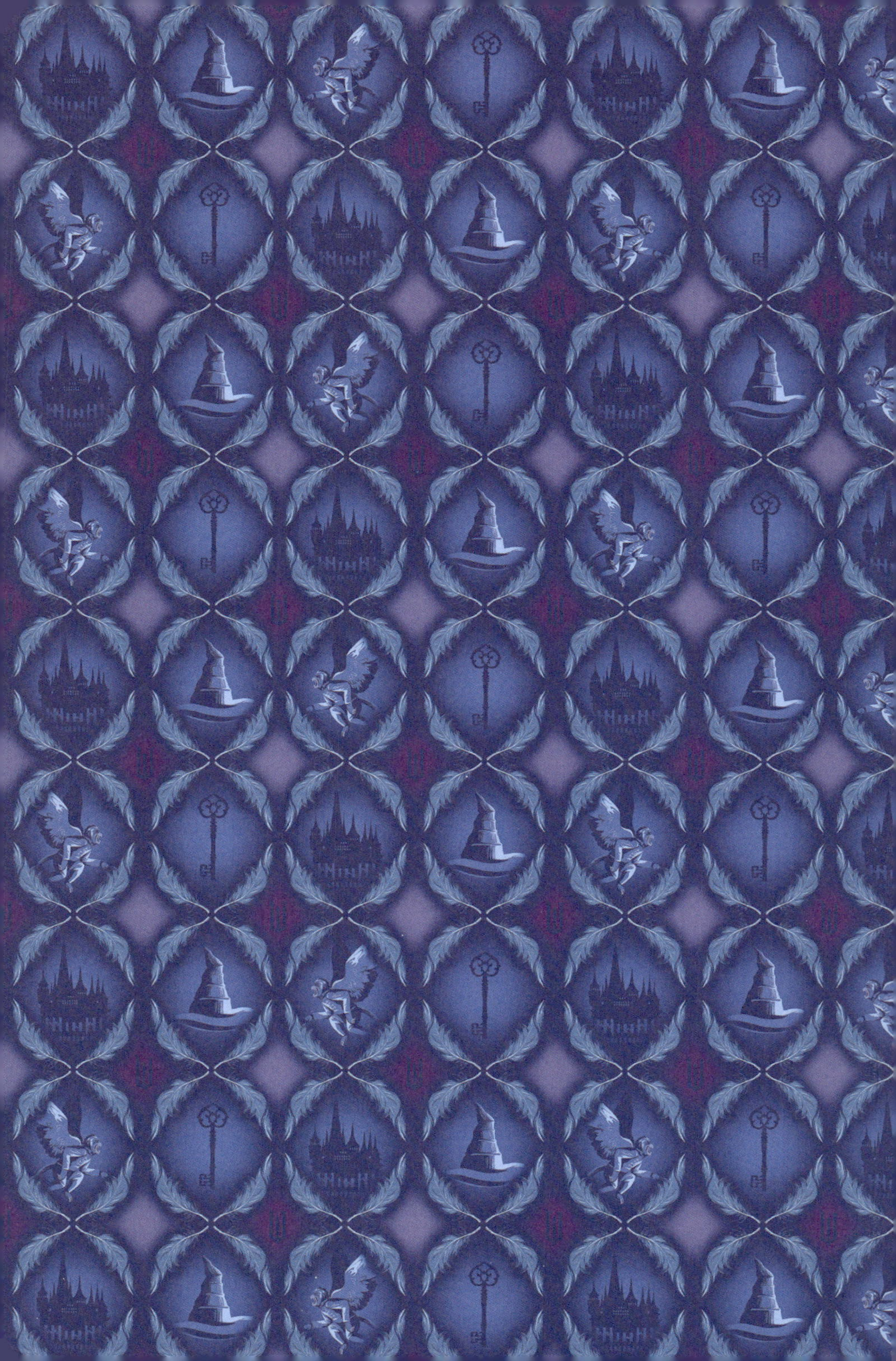